nine THE MUSICAL

Music and Lyrics by
Maury Yeston

nine
THE MUSICAL

ISBN 0-89524-820-4

Visit our website at
www.cherrylane.com

nine THE MUSICAL

Guido's Song

Lyrics and Music by
Maury Yeston

prob - lem,___ es - pe - cial - ly when my bod - y's clear - ing

for - ty as my mind is near - ing ten. I can hard - ly stay

up, and I can't get to sleep, and I don't want to

wake to - mor - row morn - ing at the bot - tom of some heap. But why

take it ___ so se - ri - ous - ly? Af - ter

all, there's noth - ing at stake here, on - ly me! I want to be

young, and I want to be old. I would like to be

wise be - fore my time, and yet be fool - ish and brash and bold. I would like the

id - i - ot went and told. I would like the u - ni - verse to get down on its knees and say

"Gui - do, what - ev - er you please, it's o - kay e - ven if it's ri - dic - u - lous, we'll ar -

range it..." SO— AR - RANGE IT!———

That's all that I want.

A Call From The Vatican

Lyrics and Music by
Maury Yeston

Swing, with a steady beat (♩=84)

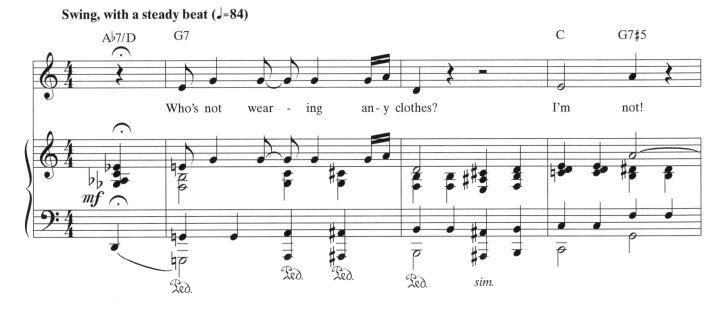

Who's not wear - ing an - y clothes? I'm not!

My dar - ling, who's a - fraid— to kiss your toes? I'm not!

Your ma - ma dear_____ is blow - ing in - to your ear,_____ so

so hot you're gon - na steam, and scream, and vi - brate like a string I'm pluck - ing, kiss your fe - vered lit - tle brow, pinch your cheeks —— till you say "ow," and I can hard - ly wait to show you how...

My Husband Makes Movies

Lyrics and Music by
Maury Yeston

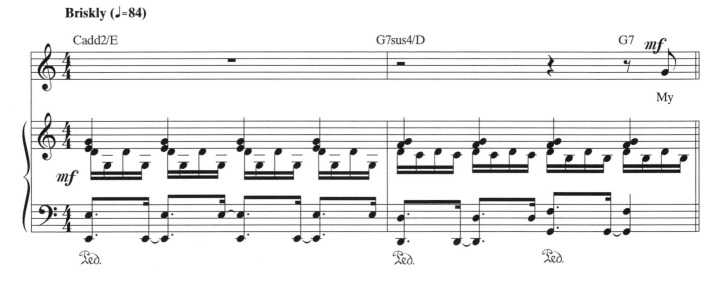

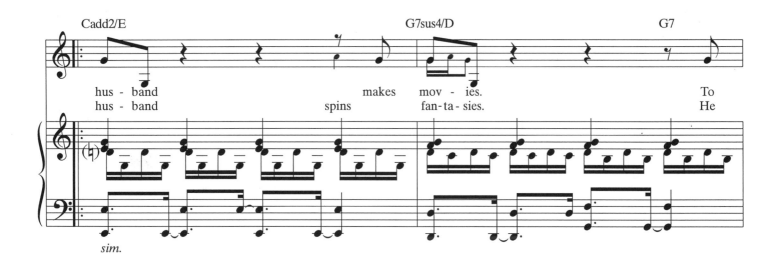

make them, he makes him-self ob-sessed. He works for

weeks on end with-out a bit of rest. No oth- er

way can he a-chieve his lev- el best.

Some men read books, some shine their shoes,

Folies Bergères

Lyrics and Music by
Maury Yeston

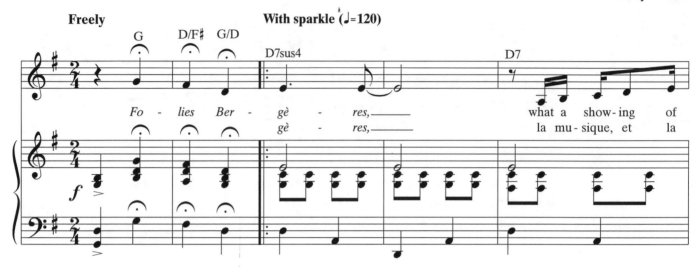

Fo - lies Ber - gè - res,_____ / gè - res,_____   what a show - ing of / la mu - sique, et la

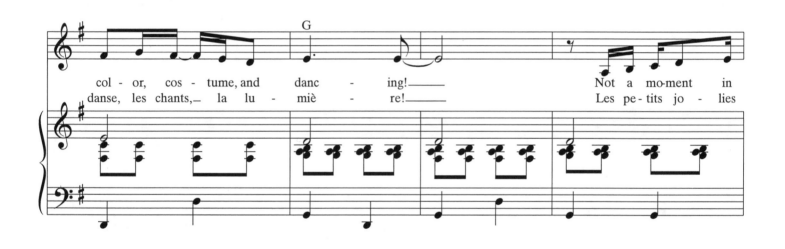

col - or, cos - tume, and danc - ing!_____ / danse, les chants,_ la lu - miè - re!_____   Not a mo - ment in / Les pe - tits jo - lies

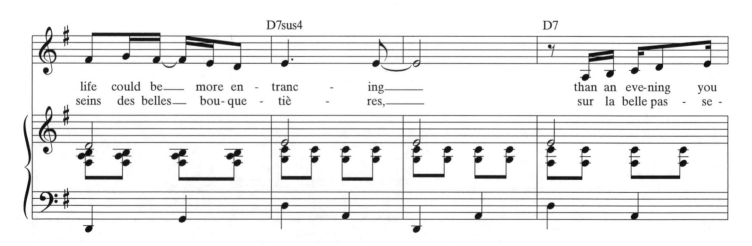

life could be_ more en - tranc - ing_____ / seins des belles_ bou - que - tiè - res,_____   than an eve - ning you / sur la belle pas - se -

spend aux *Fo - lies Ber - gè - res.*
relle des *Fo - lies Ber - gè - res.*

Fo - lies Ber - gè - res,
Fo - lies Ber - gè - res,

not a soul in the world could be___ in de - spair___
to your mod-ern i - deas, I sim - ply com - pare___

when he is glanc - ing___
one der - ri - è - re___

Only With You

Lyrics and Music by
Maury Yeston

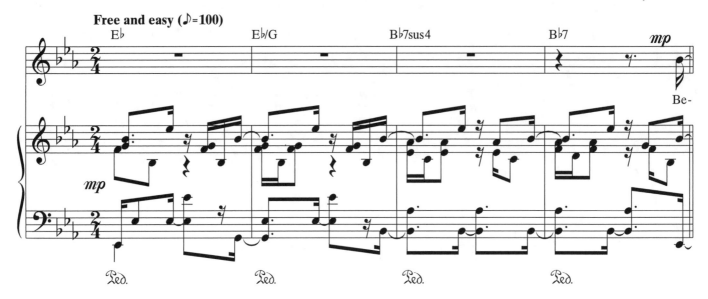

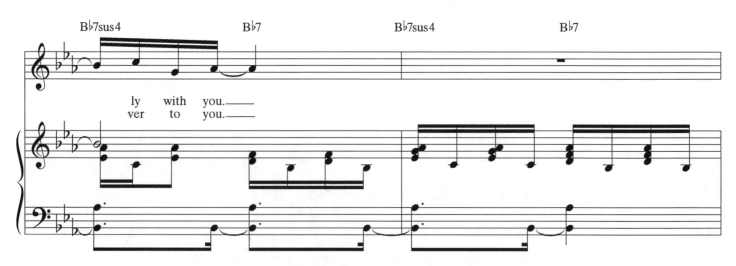

Be Italian

Lyrics and Music by
Maury Yeston

never say "Je t'aim - e," it's too pret - ty, it's good for the fran - ce - si._____ For the fran - ce - si._____ In Dutch they say "Ick lie - be," they can keep it with all the hol - lan -

learn means ev - 'ry night for you I burn "Ti vo - glio

be - ne."

"Ti vo - glio be - ne."

Now when you grow to be a man you fol - low Sa - ra - ghi - na's

be - ne." But

"Ti vo - glio be - ne."

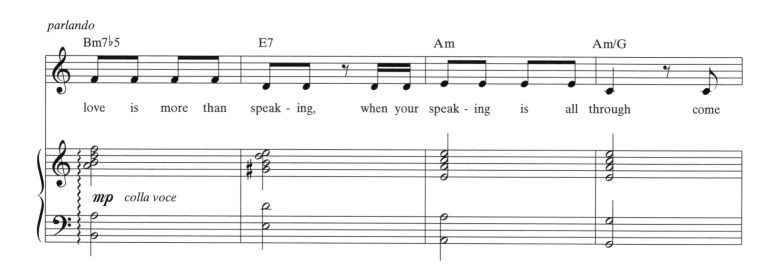

love is more than speak - ing, when your speak - ing is all through come

here a lit - tle clos - er, I will tell you what to do...

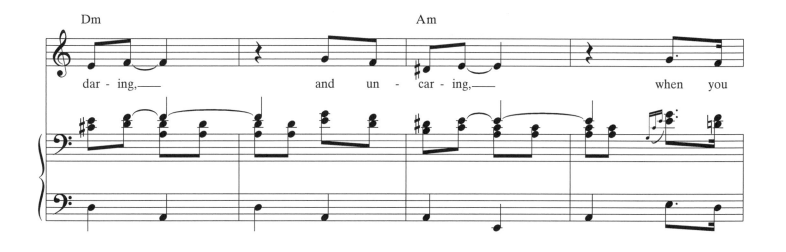

dar - ing, ___ and un - car - ing, ___ when you

pinch me try to pinch me where there's fat! Be a

sing - er! ___ Be a lov - er! ___ Pick the

Boys: Be a sing - er! ___ Be a lov - er! ___

Nine

Lyrics and Music by
Maury Yeston

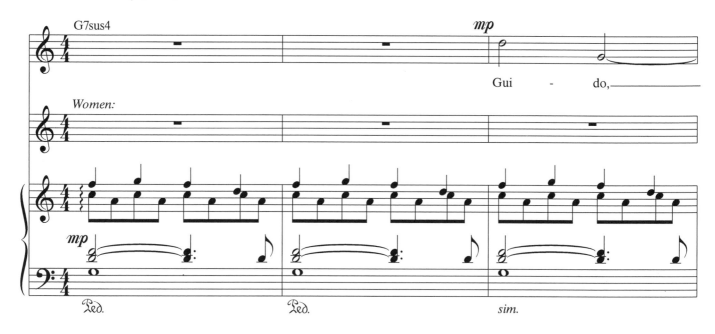

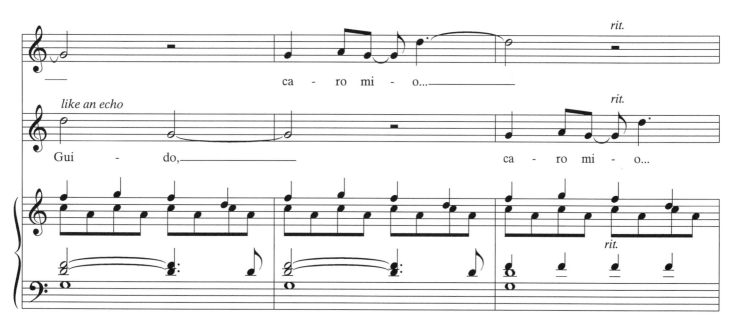

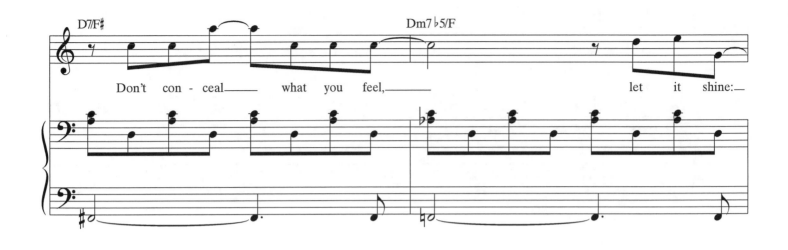

Don't con - ceal____ what you feel,____ let it shine:____

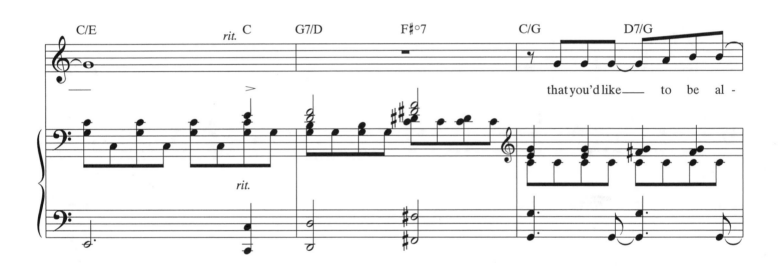

____ that you'd like____ to be al -

ways nine.

The Bells Of Saint Sebastian

Lyrics and Music by
Maury Yeston

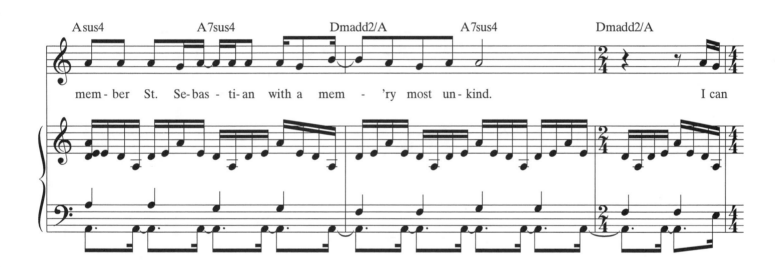

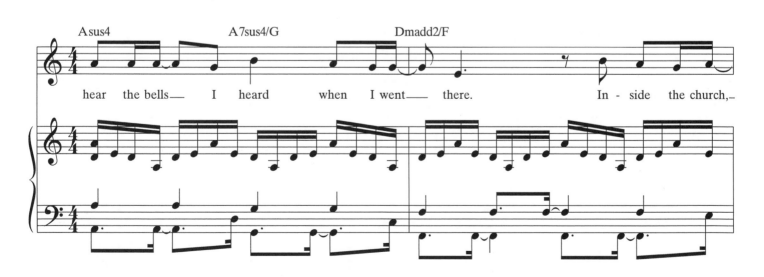

inside my mind. The bells—

— of St. Se- bas- ti- an on- ly ring once in your ears. But if—

— you're ver- y young— when you hear— them, their sound can—

Guido and Chorus:
But the

last a hun- dred years.

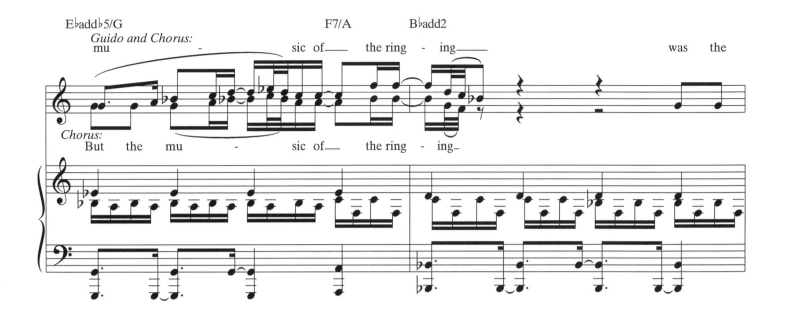

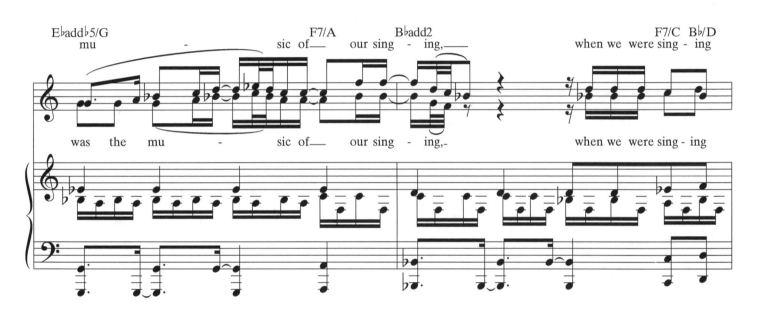

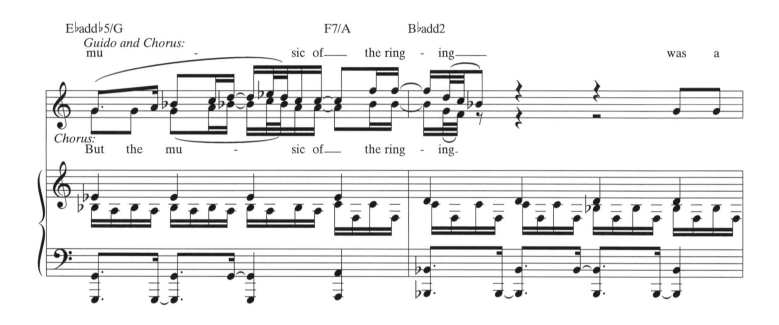

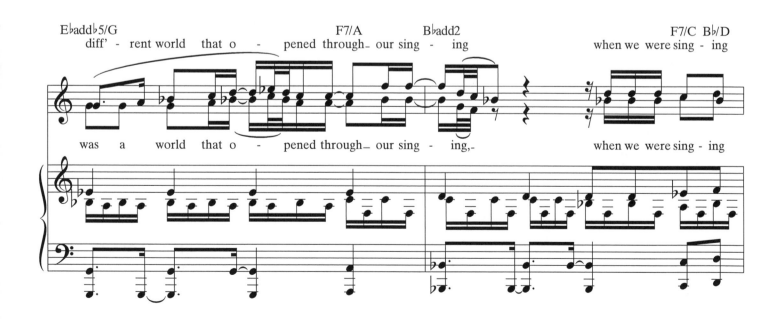

58

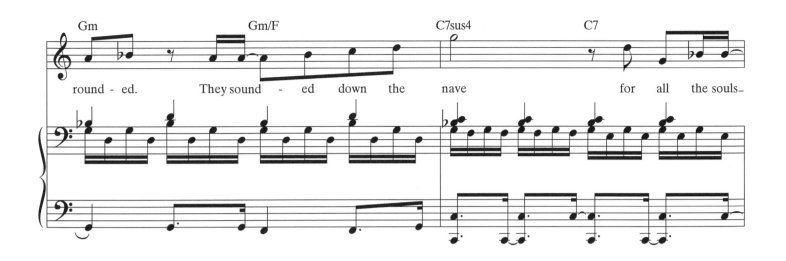

60

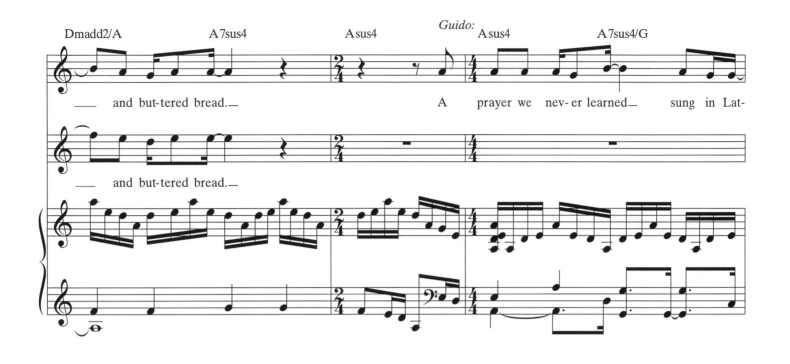

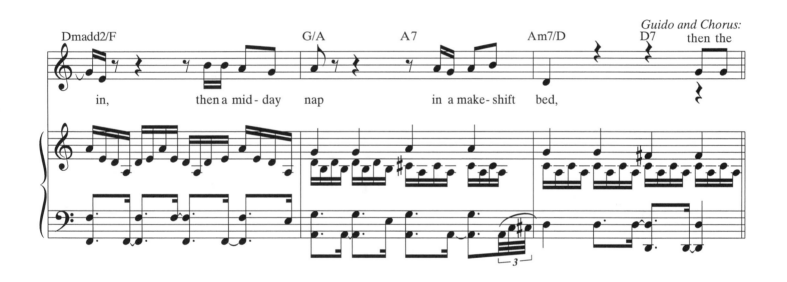

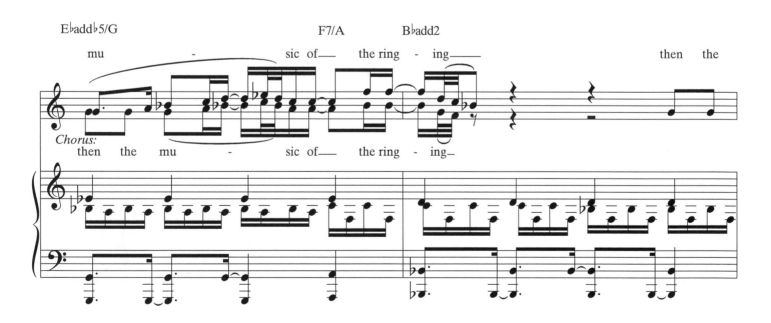

Unusual Way

Lyrics and Music by
Maury Yeston

Flowing (♩=84)

In a

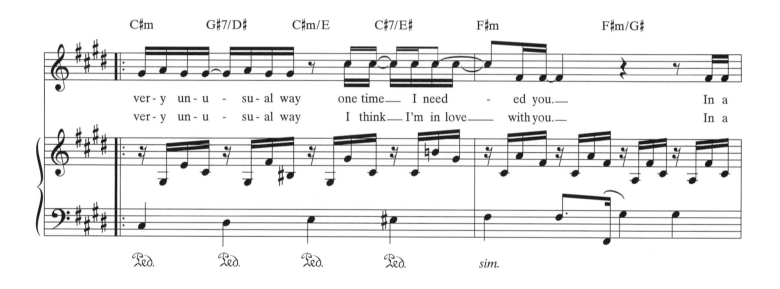

ver-y un-u-su-al way one time I need-ed you.
ver-y un-u-su-al way I think I'm in love with you.

In a

ver-y un-u-su-al way you were my friend.
ver-y un-u-su-al way I want to cry.

May - be it last - ed a day,— may - be it last - ed an hour,—
Some - thing in - side— me goes weak,— some - thing in - side— me sur - ren - ders,

1.
but some - how it will nev - er end...— In a

2.
and you're the rea - son why,— you're the rea - son— why.—

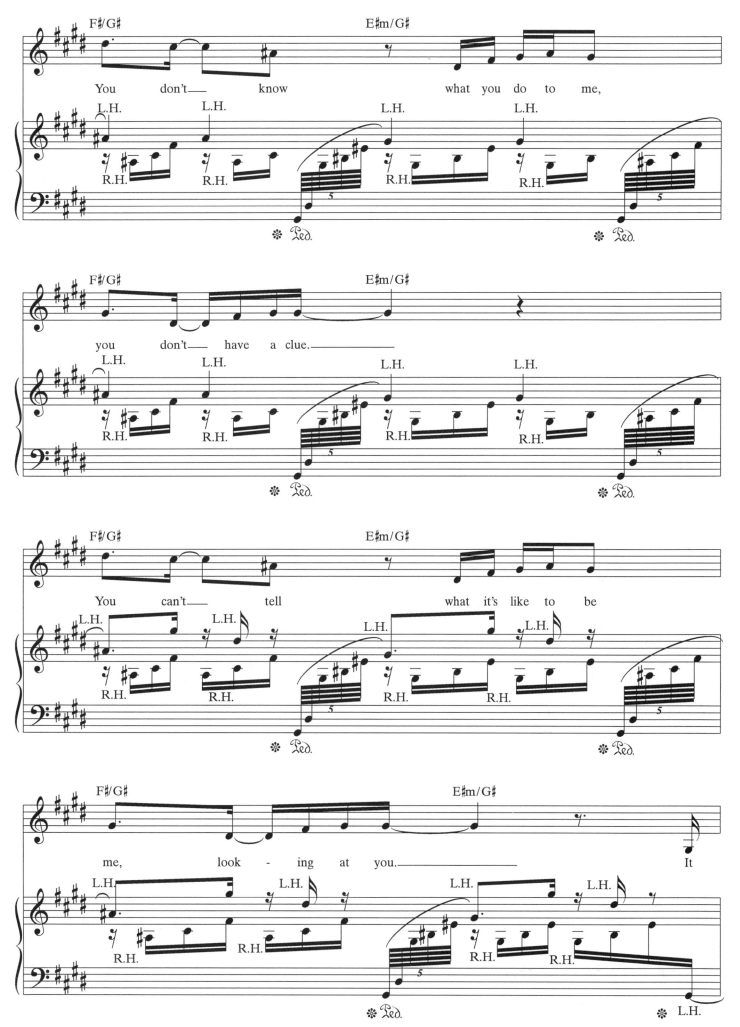

Amor

Lyrics and Music by
Maury Yeston

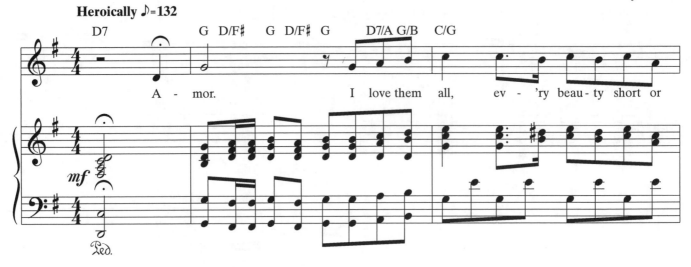

Simple

Lyrics and Music by
Maury Yeston

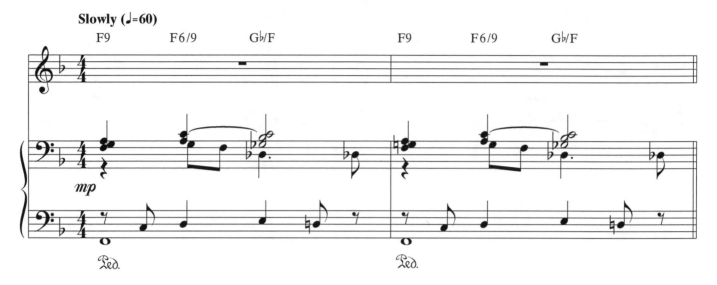

Sim - ple these af - fairs that touch the heart. Sim - ple are the ways of

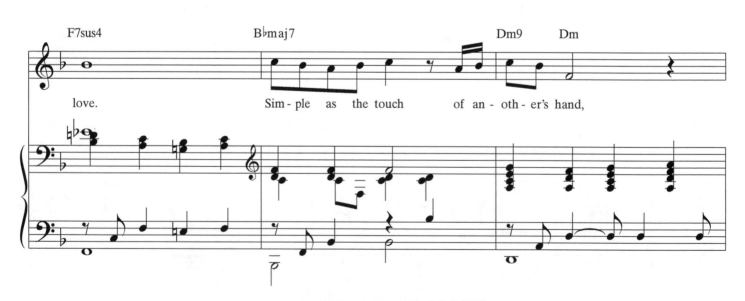

love. Sim - ple as the touch of an - oth - er's hand,

Be On Your Own

Lyrics and Music by
Maury Yeston

Driving (♩=112)

Be on your way.

There's not a sin - gle rea - son I can find to

make me want to keep you one more day.

There is - n't an - y sort of word that you could

If that is all you wish to have then I a-gree. No need for thanks, your just re-wards will be my fee. Go off and live your pet-ty fic-tions full of bla-tant con-tra-dic-tions you can't see, and what will

be   is   that   you'll leave...

and   you'll take   with you   all   you   own   from "A"   to——

"Z"   and   all   of   me.

I Can't Make This Movie

Lyrics and Music by
Maury Yeston

Waltz From Nine

Music by
Maury Yeston

Getting Tall

Lyrics and Music by
Maury Yeston

Slowly, and with feeling (♩=60)

Scrap-ing knees,___ ty - ing shoes,___ start-ing school,___

pay-ing dues,___ find-ing there's no way we can spend a life - time play-ing

ball, part of get-ting tall.

Maury Yeston

In addition to winning the Tony Award for Best Score for *Titanic* (which won the Tony for Best Musical), Maury Yeston also won the Tony and two Drama Desk Awards for his music and lyrics to Broadway's *Nine* (which won five other Tonys, including Best Musical, and was nominated for a Grammy Award and London's Olivier Award) when it first appeared on Broadway in 1982. The revival of *Nine,* starring Antonio Banderas, Chita Rivera, Jane Krakowski, Mary Stuart Masterson, and Laura Benanti, won the Tony Award for Best Revival in 2003, with a cast album released by PS Classics. His work on Broadway's *Grand Hotel* was also nominated for a Tony and two Drama Desk Awards.

Yeston's music and lyrics cover a variety of styles and are showcased in *The Maury Yeston Songbook* (PS Classics)—a collection of his finest work, recorded by a group of celebrated Broadway stars. His Cello Concerto was premiered by Yo-Yo Ma, while his album *Goya—A Life in Song* featured Placido Domingo and Gloria Estefan and included the song "Till I Loved You," subsequently a Top 40 Barbra Streisand hit. His classical crossover *December Songs* was commissioned by Carnegie Hall for its centennial celebration and recorded on RCA Records. Other Yeston works recorded on RCA Records include the score to his *Phantom,* which has received national and international acclaim, and the London Concert version of *Nine,* which starred Jonathan Pryce and Elaine Paige.

In 2000 he was commissioned by the Kennedy Center for the Performing Arts to compose *An American Cantata for 2000 Voices*—a choral symphony in three movements, which premiered on the steps of the Lincoln Memorial by the National Symphony Orchestra under the baton of Leonard Slatkin.

In June 2003 he premiered his new book and musical adaptation of Frank Loesser's *Hans Christian Andersen,* now scheduled for worldwide production.

Yeston serves as Director of the BMI Music Theatre Workshop in New York City and is also the President of the Kleban Foundation. He holds a BA and MA from both Yale University and Clare College, Cambridge, as well as a Ph.D. from Yale, where he was a member of the faculty for eight years as Director of Undergraduate Studies in Music.

More Great Piano/Vocal Books from Cherry Lane

For a complete listing of Cherry Lane titles available, including contents listings, please visit our web site at
www.cherrylane.com

See your local music dealer or contact:

CHERRY LANE MUSIC COMPANY
6 East 32nd Street, New York, NY 10016

EXCLUSIVELY DISTRIBUTED BY

HAL•LEONARD® CORPORATION
7777 W. BLUEMOUND RD. P.O. BOX 13819 Milwaukee, WI 53213

Prices, contents and availability subject to change without notice.